esoteric thinking

The
The
The

By Nader Bolour

Old...
New...
Future!

Monograph

The Old

Finding unique and timeless rugs has always been a challenge, more so now, to suit modern interiors and the taste of younger designers and architects who now cater to a younger clientele. The challenge allows us to break new grounds and envision antique rugs in a different light. This chapter is a glimpse into my ongoing search for uniqueness and innovation.

Nader Bolour

BB6112 Persian Kashan 11'3" × 8'5"

BB6068 Deco 10' × 5'9"

BB6100 Turkish Oushak 14' × 11'

BB5995 Turkish Oushak 16'9" × 13'9"

BB6053 A turkish Oushak 9' × 6'1'

BB6102 Turkish Oushak 15'3" × 11'10"

BB6134 Persian Sultanabad 12'6" × 9'6"

BB6094 Samarkand 13'7" × 7'

BB5191 Indian Amritsar 9'4 " × 7'9"

BB6144 French Deco 11' × 7'7"

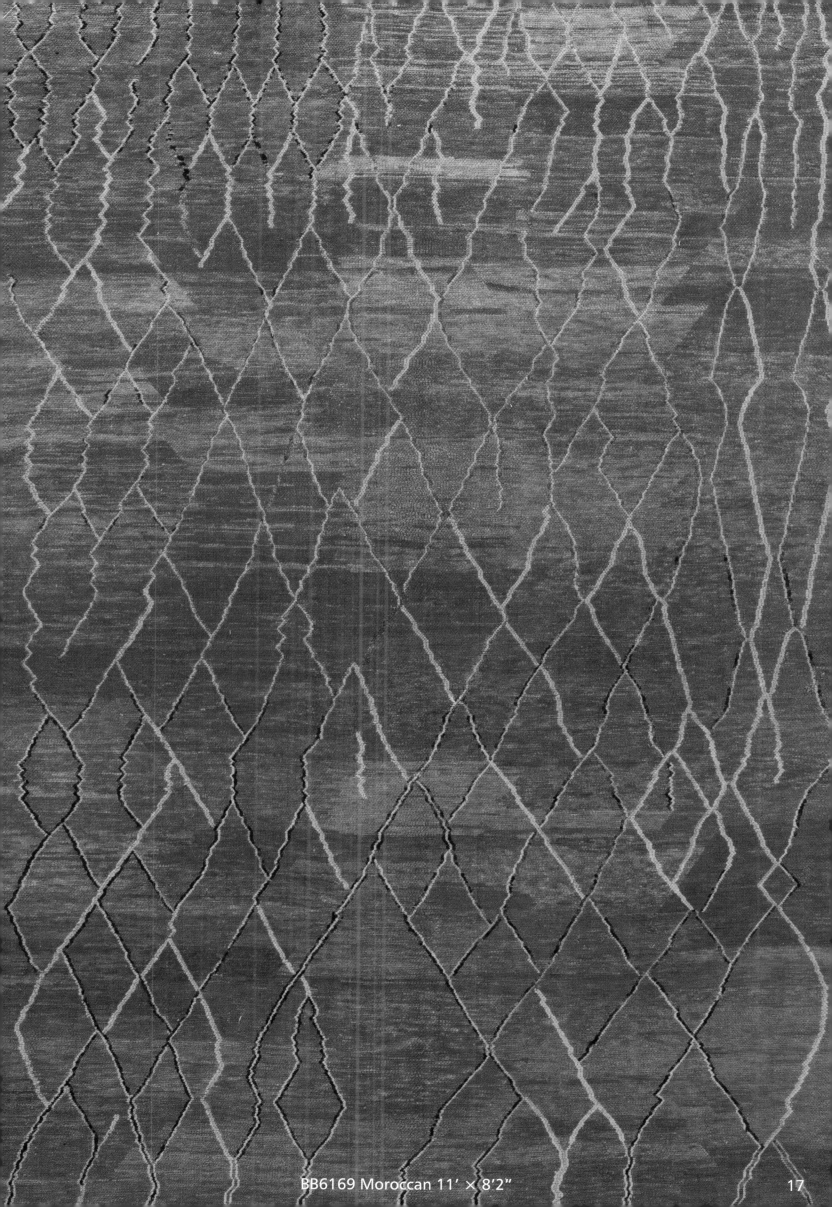

BB6169 Moroccan 11' × 8'2"

BB5970 Persian Tabriz 11'4" × 8'2"

BB5187 Arts & Crafts by C.F.A. Voysey 9'2" × 6'10"

BB6122 Swedish Flatweave Signed SH (Svensk Hemslöjd) 8'8" × 5'8"

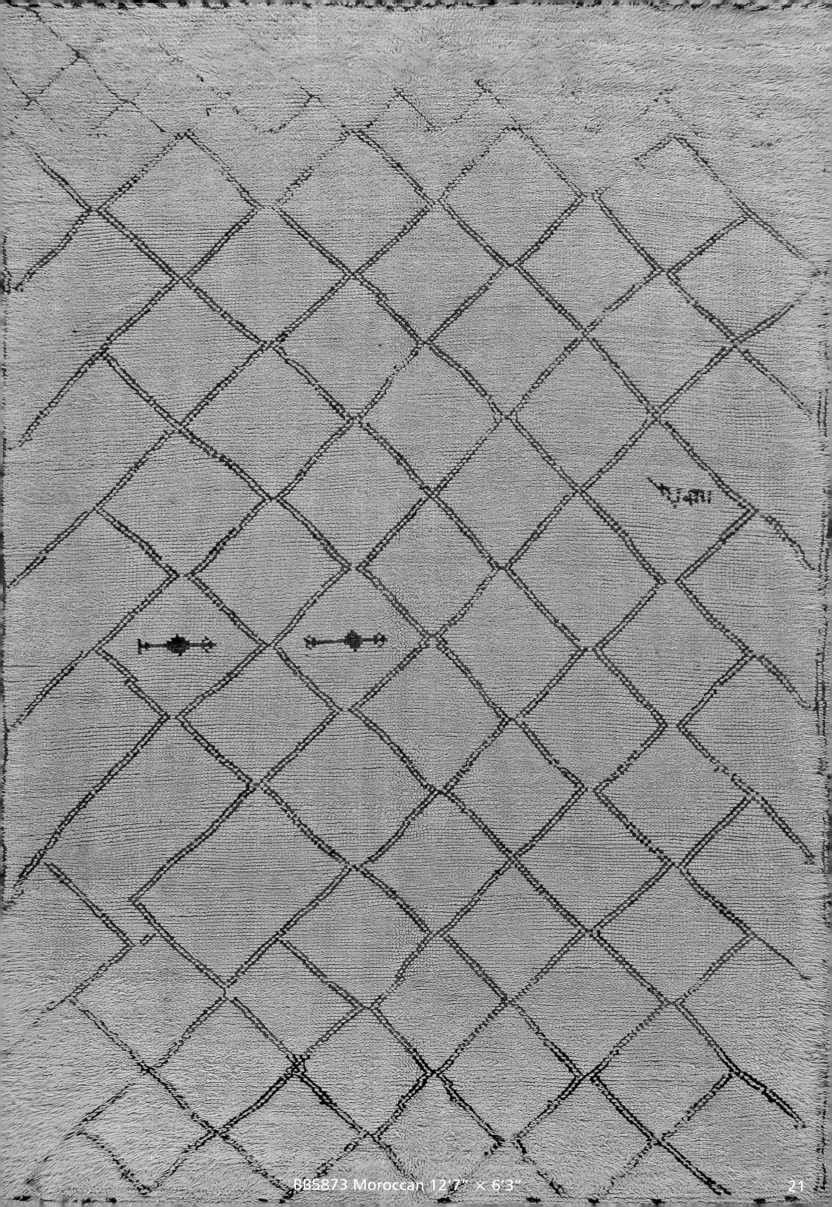

BB4499 Samarkand 17'7" × 8'9"

BB6059 Persian Khorassan 16'6" × 11'4"

BB5211 Aubusson 12'2" × 11'2"

BB6036 Bessarabian 12'4" × 11'8"

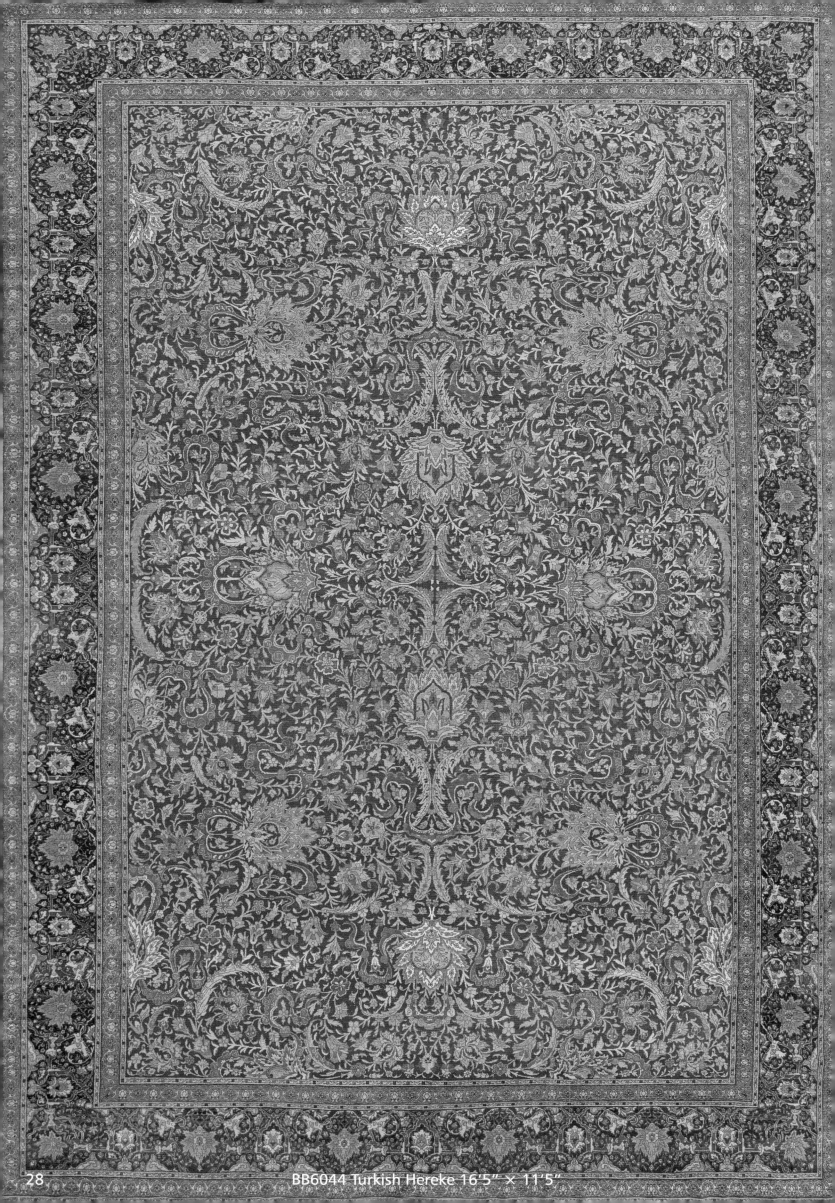

BB6044 Turkish Hereke 16'5" × 11'5"

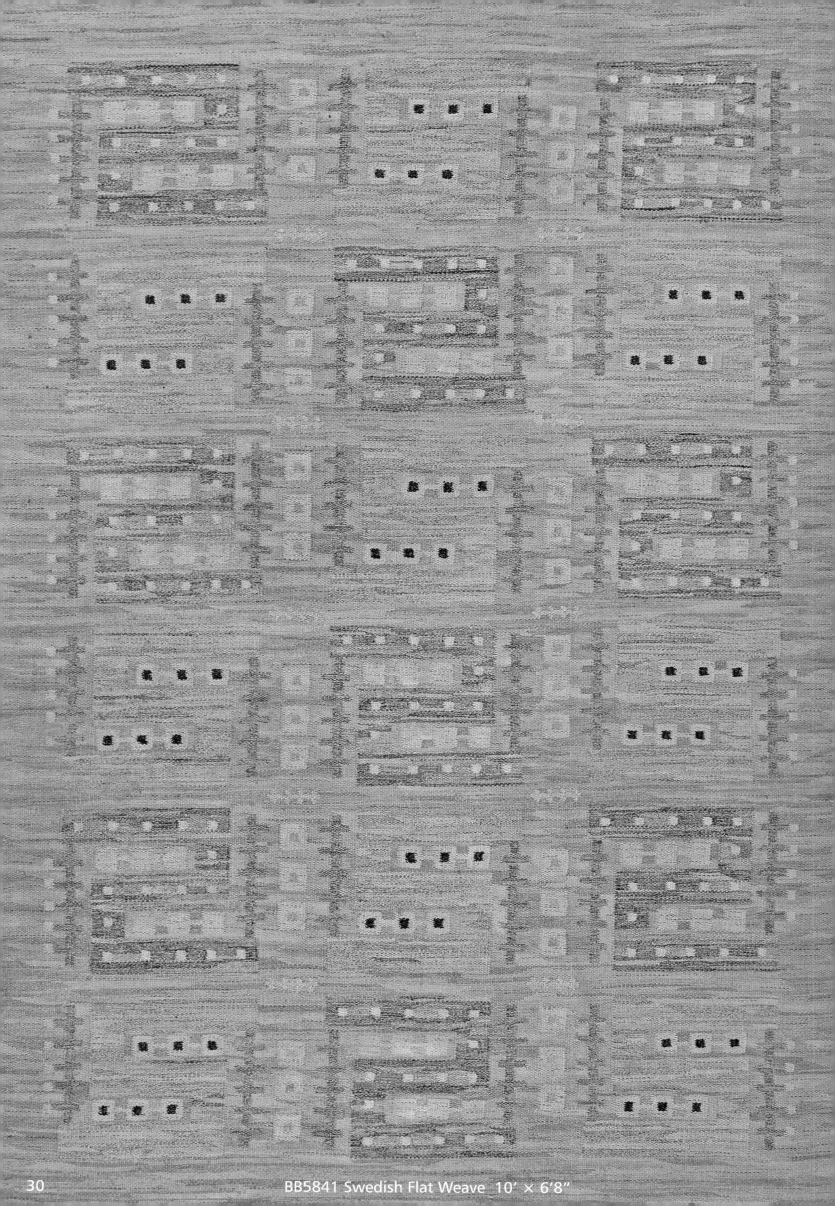

BB5841 Swedish Flat Weave 10' × 6'8"

BB5163 Aubusson 21'10" × 13'8"

BB5744 Chinese 10'2" × 5'10"

BB5254 Swedish Flatweave 13'9" × 9'9"

BB5462 Indian Amritsar 17'3" × 14'3"

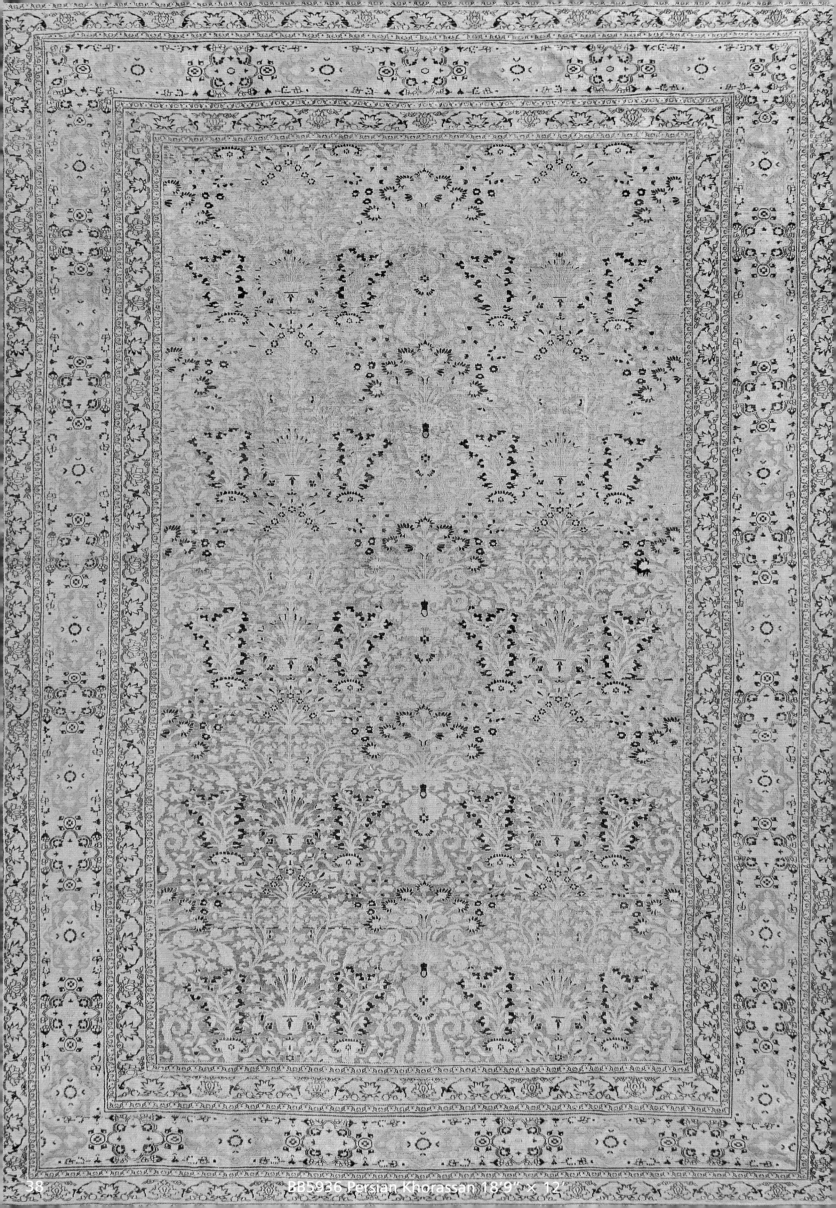

BB5936 Persian Khorassan 18'9" × 12'

BB5885 Persian Kirman 15'10" × 11'10"

BB6132 Persian Kirman 21'3" × 14'10"

BB3679 Chinese Deco 17'3 " × 10'7"

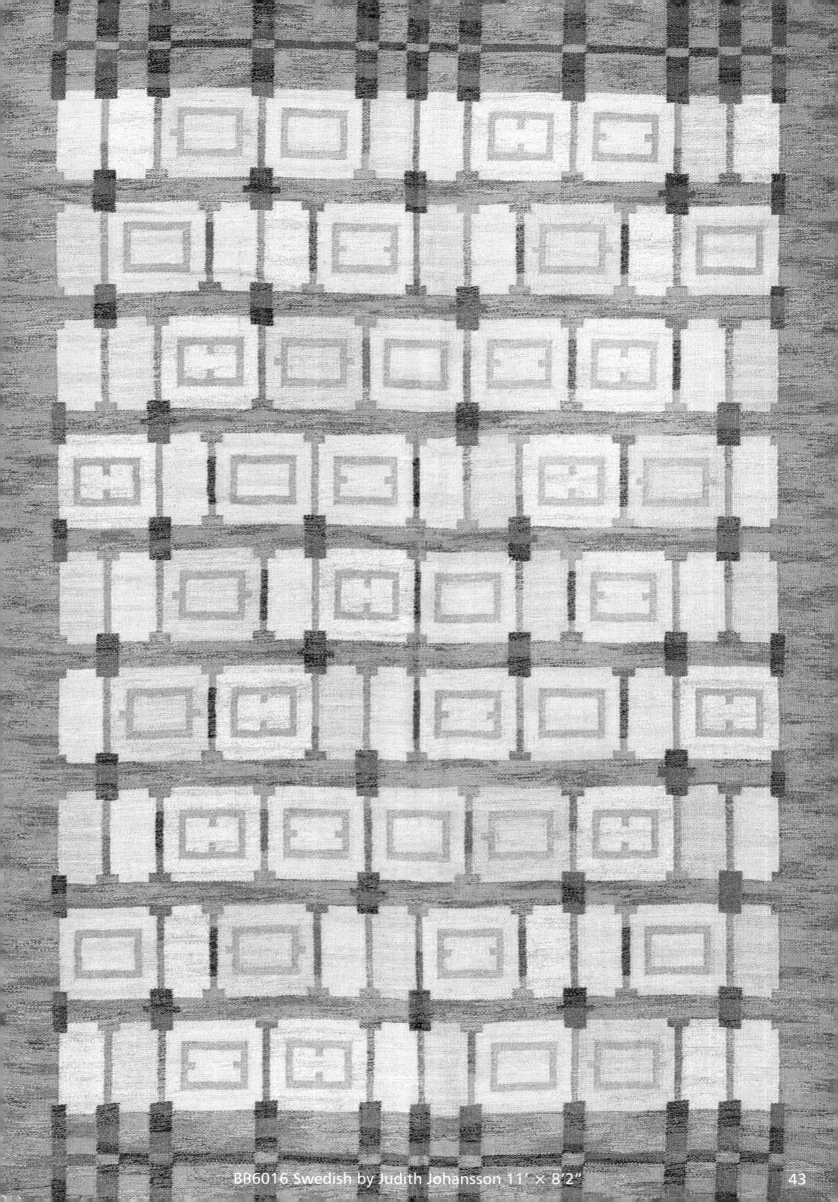

BB6039 Moroccan 10' & 7'

BB5832 Art Deco 11' × 8'

The New

Evolving Further!

Blue Stripes 12" × 9"

N11203 14'9" × 9'10"

N10931 14'10" × 12'1"

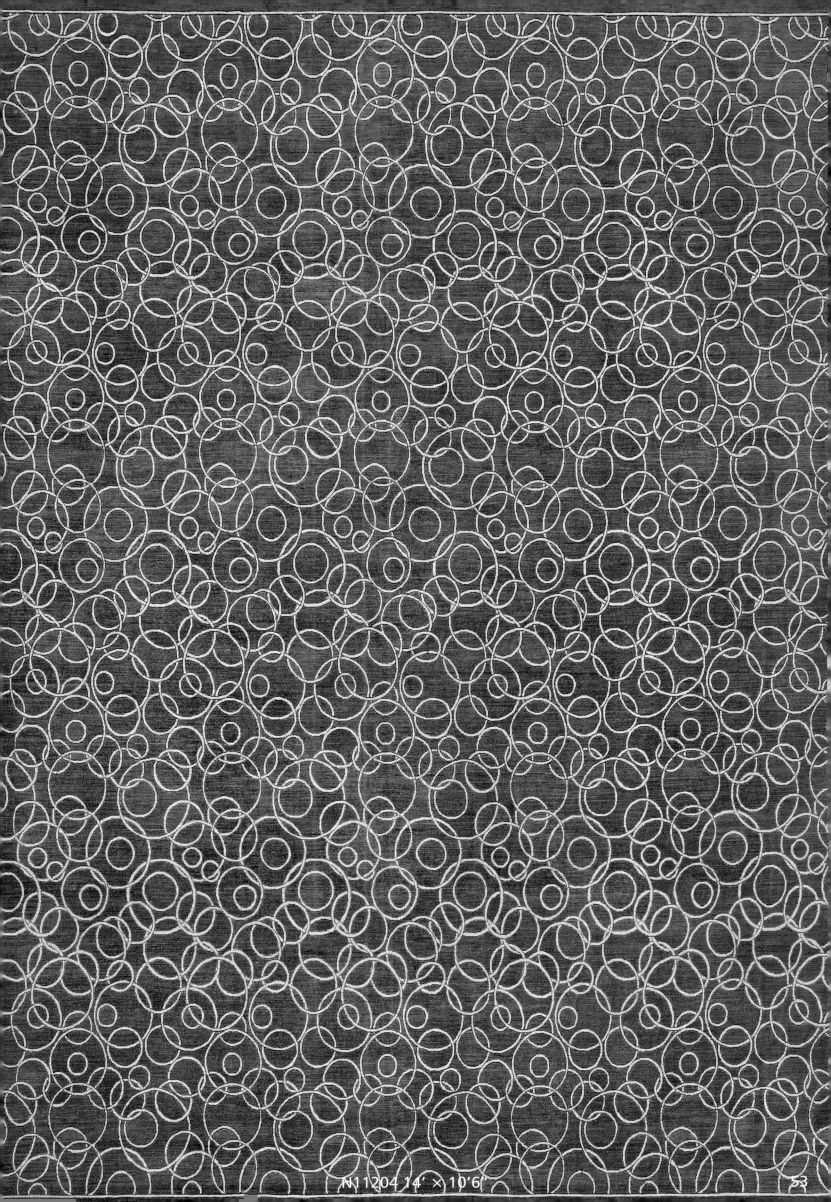

Mikos 12' x 9'

Ink 17' x 13'

Sketch 16" x 13"

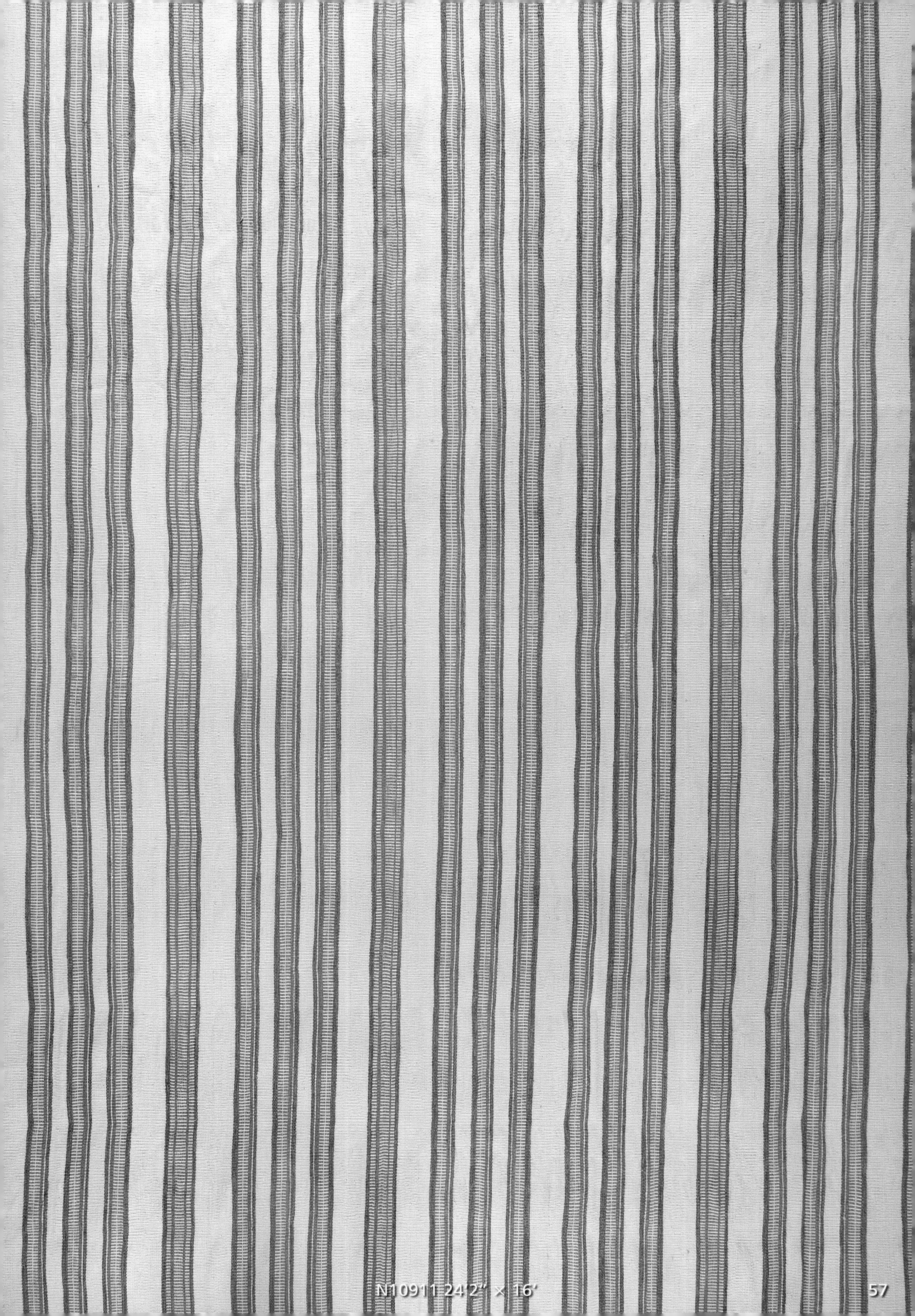

N10911 24'2" × 16'

Color Drop 15' x 12'

Traces 15' × 10'

N10779 24' × 14'4"

N11191 21' × 13'

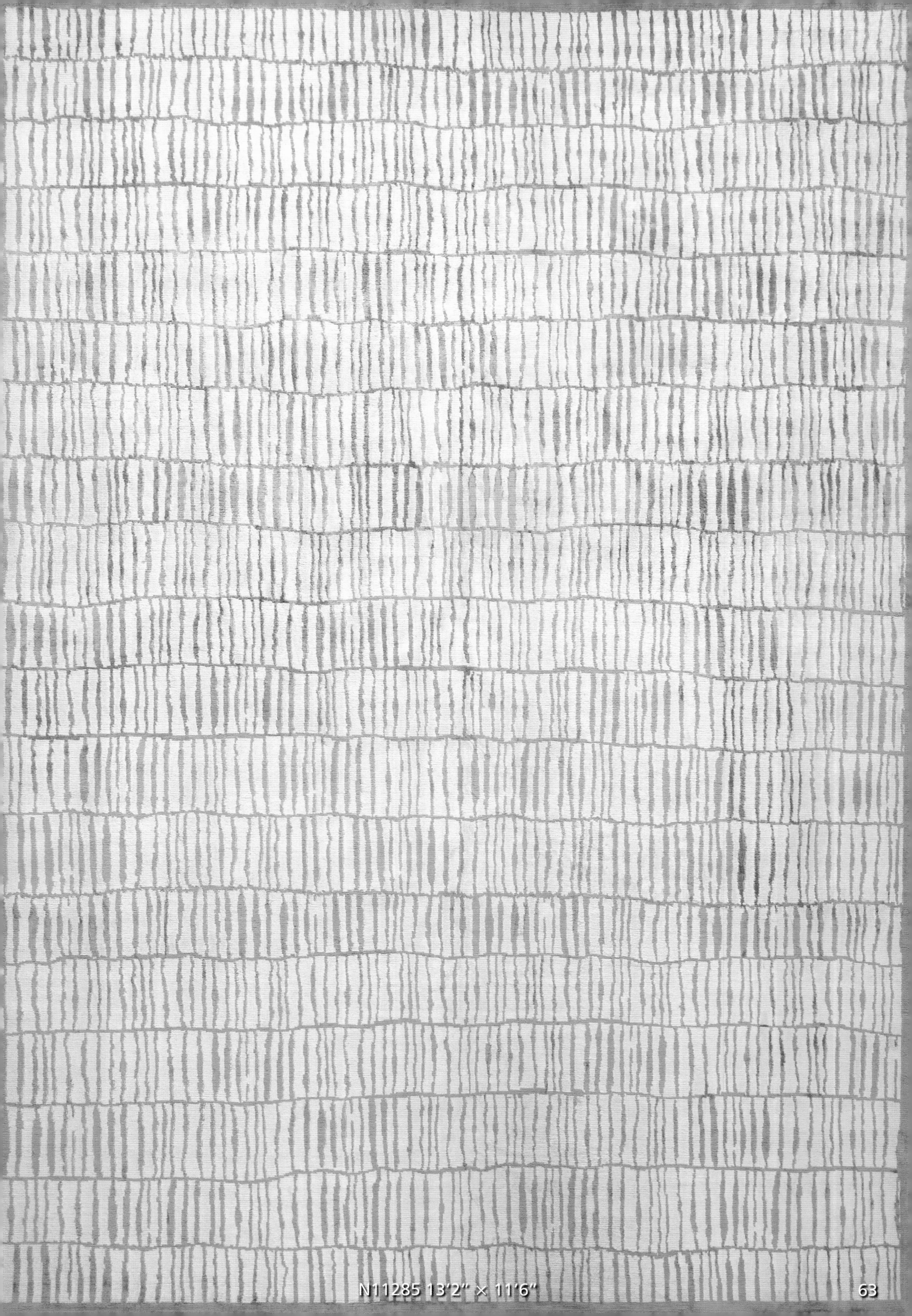

N11285 13'2" × 11'6"

N11255 18'2" × 12'

N11286 21' × 14'

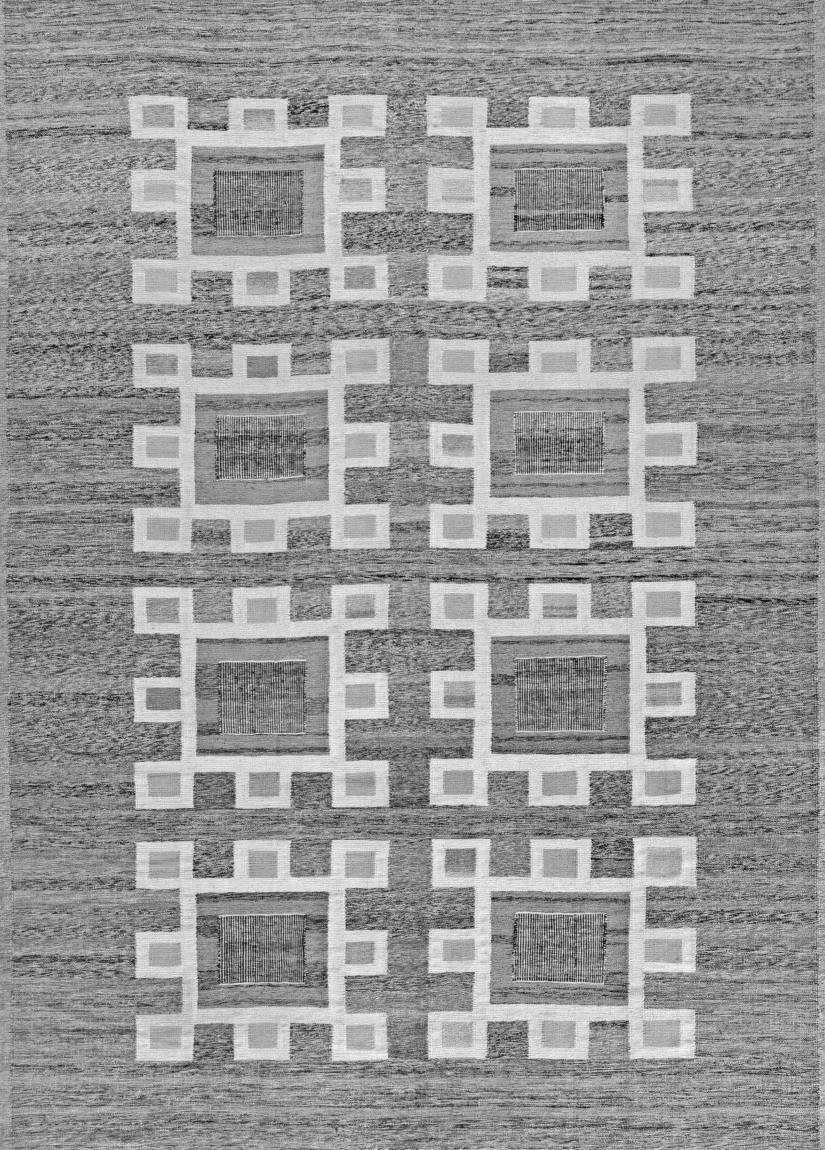

N11206 14'7" × 9'10"

N11303 13'7" x 12'10"

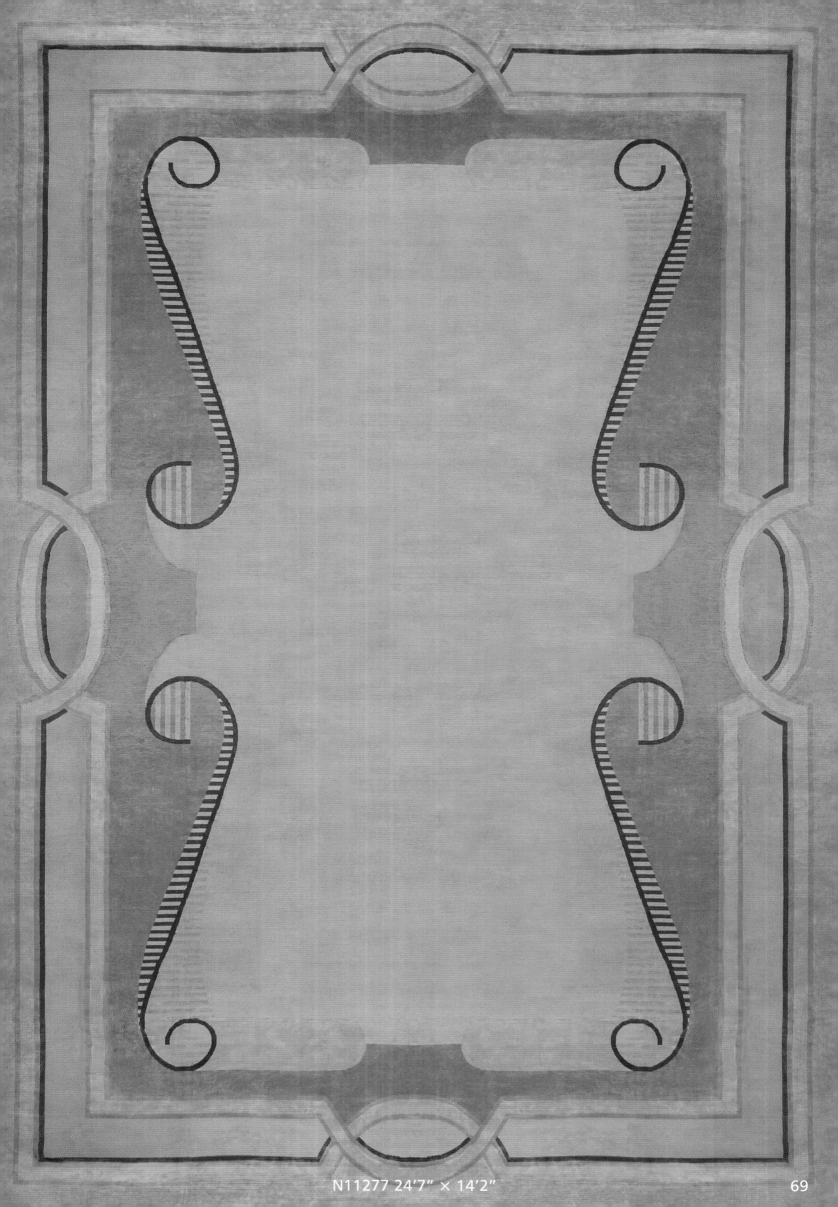

N11277 24'7" × 14'2"

N11133 15'10" × 13'

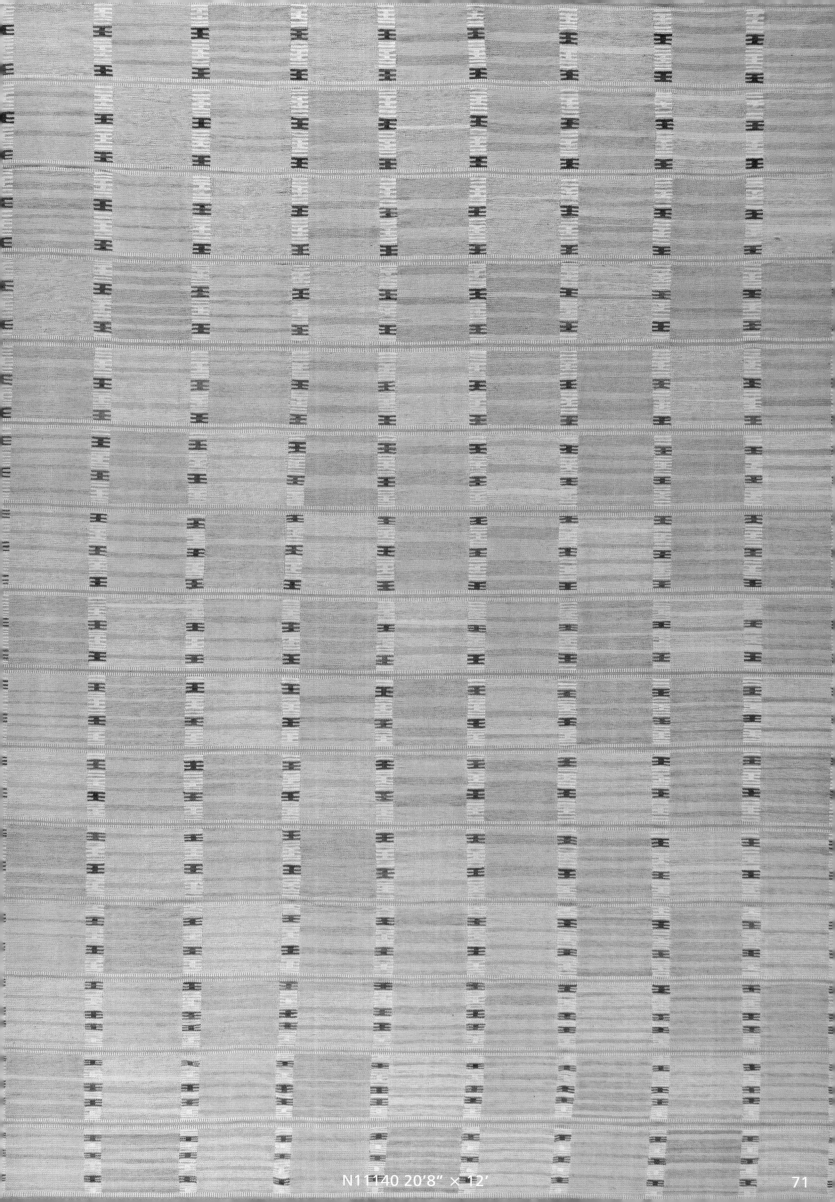

N11305 17' × 13'

73

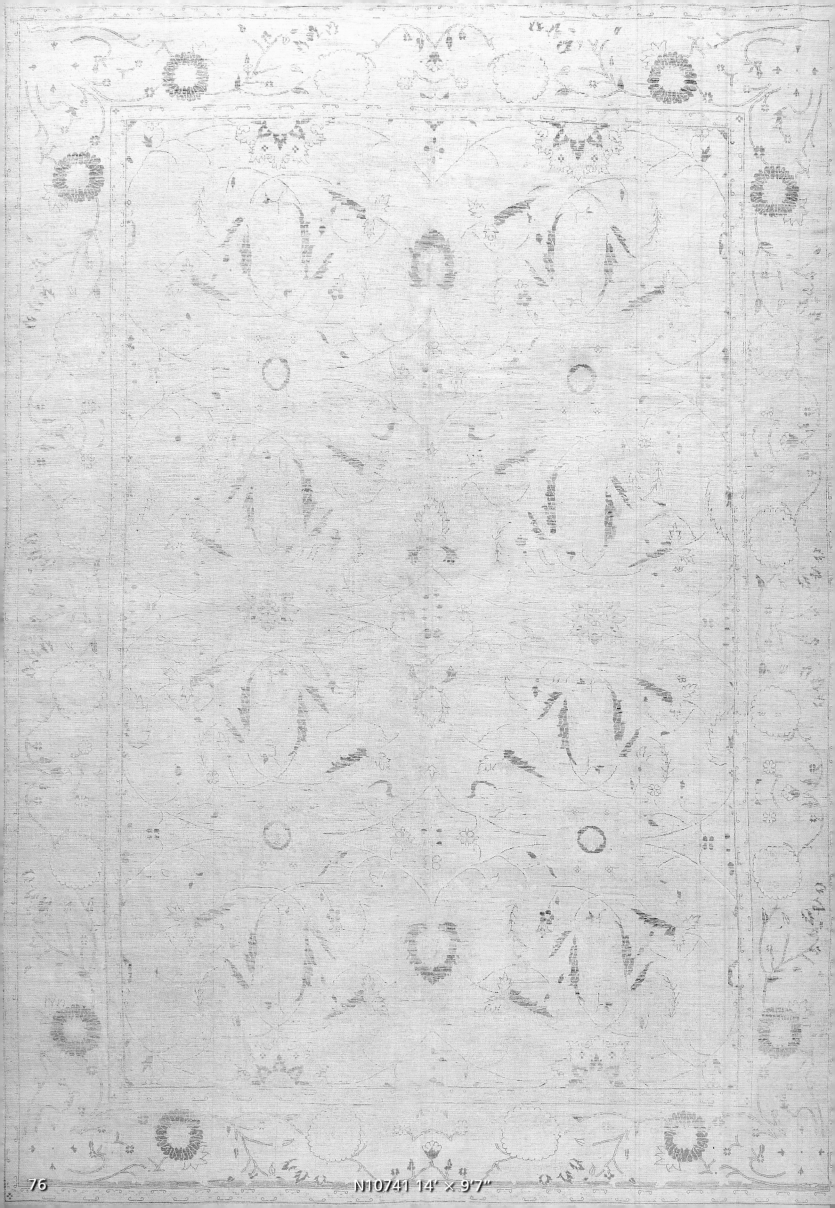

N10741 14' × 9'7"

Silvery 12' × 9'

N11201 10'3" × 9'

N10839 12' × 9'

Spheres 18' × 13'

Future

Our excitement comes from the knowledge of not knowing. The mystery of this is enticing and rewarding.

Our reward comes in the surprise in what will happen and how we will adapt our existing and color palette to it.

As the Creative Director, I cannot wait to see how it unfolds.

Suzan Izsak

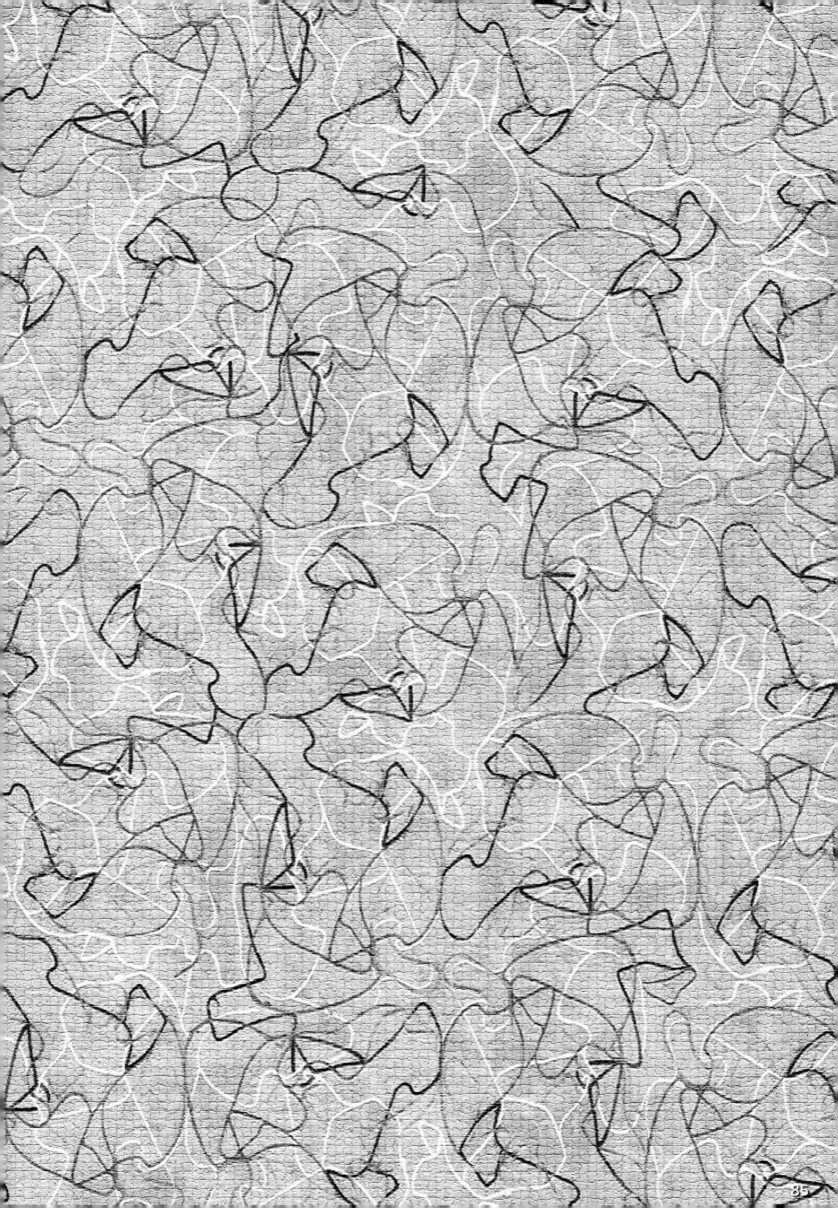

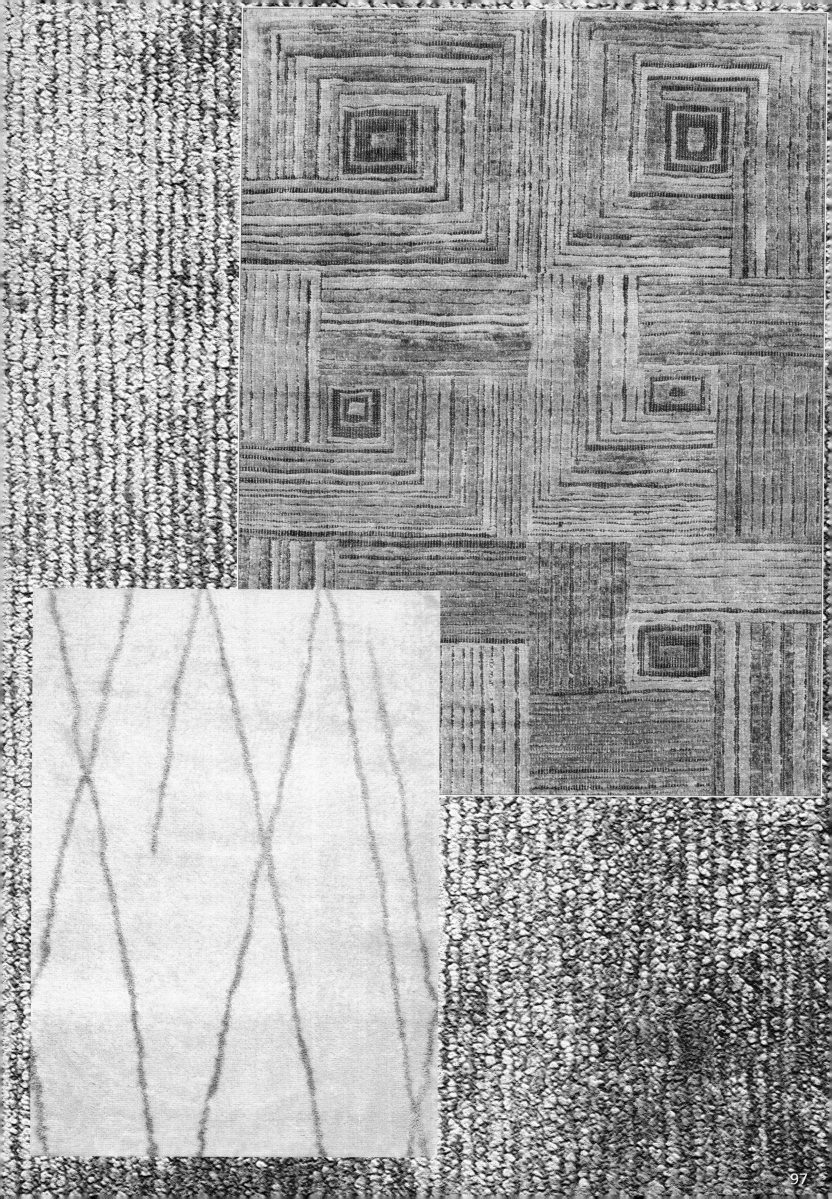

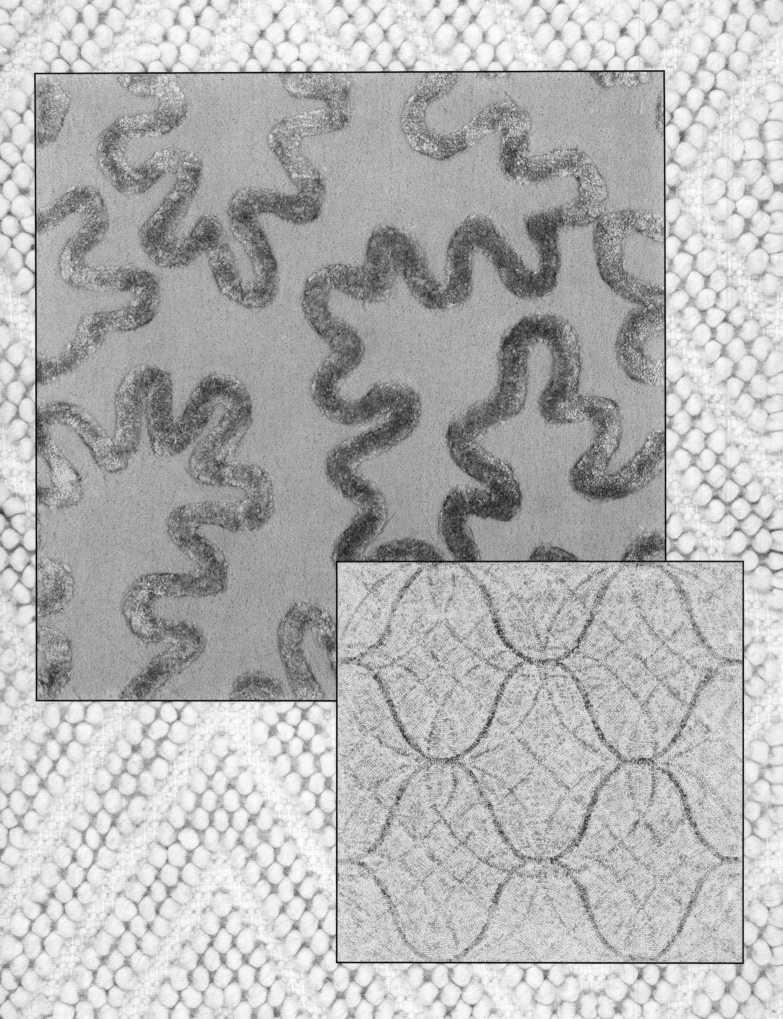

Doris Leslie Blau

MAIN SHOWROOM   306 E. 61st Street, 7th Floor, New York, NY 10065

D&D BUILDING   979 3rd Avenue, Suite 625, New York, NY 10022

Washington Design Center   1099 14th Street NW, Suite 325, Washington, DC 20005

Tel. 212-586-5511   Email: nader@dorisleslieblau.com

www.dorisleslieblau.com

$39.99

ISBN 978-1-4951-9297-5

MAGRAF s.c., Bydgoszcz

Printed by ABEDIK, Bydgoszcz